ABBOT'S
RABBIT
Written by Patricia "Pat" Hagan
Artwork & Design by Jordan Hancock

AuthorHouse™
1663 Liberty Drive
Bloomington, IN 47403
www.authorhouse.com
Phone: 1 (800) 839-8640

Published by AuthorHouse 10/06/2017

ISBN: 978-1-5462-0771-9 (sc)
ISBN: 978-1-5462-0773-3 (hc)
ISBN: 978-1-5462-0772-6 (e)

Library of Congress Control Number: 2017913934

Print information available on the last page.

authorHOUSE®

Thanks Robert, for the inspiration
of a story that will inspire others
to look, listen, and learn!

Patricia (Pat) Hagan has written this story for you.
She has had lots of time to think about many things
including land and sea and sky,
and the creatures who live there - both those she saw
and maybe those who were invisible.
Most of her childhood she spent rowing and
sailing on the Charles River or
exploring the greenery along its banks.
It was a childhood filled with wonder and joy.
Pat didn't just look and listen,
she stored those sights and sounds away
in her thoughts along with her imagined stories.
As time passed, she often told those stories to children
she counseled at camp in the summer or
those who came to her for their piano lessons.
Now it's time to give you one of those stories - in a book!
That's special, and so is that Rabbit!

Hi! I'm Jordan Hancock,
the artist for the illustrations in this story of
Abbot's Rabbit.
Here is how that happened.
One day "Pat" was busy writing down her thoughts.
When I asked what she was thinking about she told me
about a story book she was planning to write for children.
Then she told the story to me. As she spoke I imagined
the boy, Abbot, and then his friends, the animals, and then
the scenes of their activities. It all came alive for me,
so I offered to create illustrations for her story,
to make Abbot's Rabbit super enjoyable for
you today and every day that you read it,
or just even look at it,
or whistle,
or play,
or sing Abbot's Song.
Keep smiling!!

Welcome to the world of Abbot and Rabbit.
It is such a happy place where the wonder
of friendship can happen when you look
and listen carefully.
Are you ready?
We're ready to tell you
how it happened to Abbot.

Contents

Chapter 1 Here come the Birds

Abbot always loved animals. He loved animals of all sizes, but especially small ones. He spent time in the city

and also time in the country, and he noticed wherever he went he saw birds.

Sometimes they stood there very still, but even then they would still move their heads up-and-down and left and -right. Sometimes they walked around while they were moving their heads, and sometimes quite suddlenly they would spread their wings, lift themselves up and start to fly away.

They would fly high, sometimes high up into the trees, and sometimes fly far away until he couldn't see them anymore. Abbot thought - "Birds are like magic, and I wonder if they get very hungry having such busy days".

Abbot had seen people feeding birds, and decided he would feed birds too with food he would buy at the pet store.

He could hardly wait to get back home and take some of his savings to get ready for a trip to the pet store.

Chapter 2 Chipmunk Comes To Visit

Soon Abbot had some bird friends in the city. He carried a little bag of birdseed with him whenever he went to the park, hoping he would see his friends so he could feed them.

In the country he noticed that the birds were eating little bits and pieces, which fell from the leaves and plants in the woods. So Abbot had to pay more attention to the birds in the city who needed the food Abbot was carrying.

He even got a little feeder which he put near his door and placed some seeds in it for the birds. Then – guess what! One day another small animal came to enjoy the birdseed and the company!

Abbot recognized him as a chipmunk - from pictures he had seen in his book. That was a long name for such a little friend, so Abbot thought of him right away as "Chipper".

He didn't know whether the chipmunk was eating the birdseed or taking it with him to save up for the winter. Whatever Chipper was doing, Abbot knew he would have to feed him since he wanted to be friendly with the birds.

Abbot's little group was growing and it was making him happy – happier than he had been for a while! "What an interesting group", he thought.

Abbot knew that birds like to fly way above the ground and chipmunks like to burrow - that means they like to dig tunnels and travel around much of the time underground. They must be like mechanics or engineers! Abbot thought he couldn't be happier!

Chapter 3 Bird and Chipper make a Plan

Many birds came and went to and from the feeder, and they were all good friends to each other and to Abbot. But the first Bird who came was the friendliest toward Abbot and also chirped and sang more often than any of the others.

Chipper was very different, although sometimes he made sounds like a little bird. Also, of course, he couldn't fly like the birds so he would scurry here and there and would like to burrow near the house sometimes.

But Bird would tell him not to do that because it could be bad for the house, and told him to go back to the woods if he wanted to burrow. Chipper could make very long tunnels, as long as 30 feet!

Although they were quite different, Bird and Chipper were good friends to each other and both of them loved Abbot. They both thought that Abbot needed another friend who would be kind and sweet and gentle – a friend he could even bring into his house.

From time to time they would see what looked like two white ears or maybe brown ears showing between the blades of grass, or between the leaves, or from behind a tree.

They knew that those most certainly must be ears of rabbits, those kind sweet gentle creatures that would be great for Abbot.

Chipper was ready to dig a long burrow out to the nicest rabbit they could find, have a talk with, and invite and bring him to lunch. This way Chipper could get to rabbit without frightening him with any noise.

They were very proud of their plan. Now they had to teach Abbot the surprise song and also find food for Rabbit's lunch.

Chapter 4  Planning for Rabbit

Chipper now knew his part of the plan and agreed that he was ready to start digging over to the tree in the wooded area to see that rabbit was ready to talk to him.

Bird agreed to perform a quite different task, and said he could do it because, as everyone knows, birds can sing - so they must know a lot about music!

He would write a song for Abbot to sing to Rabbit, and Chipper would write the words, if he wanted to. Abbot could even play the song for Rabbit on his recorder which he learned to play at school. What a plan!

Well, best of all, the day came when Rabbit arrived for lunch with Bird and lots of birds, and with Chipper, and guess what Rabbit brought along - a carrot in his mouth! His lunch!!

They all dropped their food for a few minutes and they laughed and laughed, and Abbot laughed with them. What a happy day!

And here's a happy surprise...... look at the next chapter to see the song that Bird and Chipper wrote for Abbot to play for and sing to Rabbit! Remember: You can sing it and play it too, just like Abbot!

Chapter 5 Abbot's Song

LIT-TLE BIRDS SING OUT TWEET TWEET TWEET

LOOK LOOK THEY'RE DAN-CING ON TI-NY FEET

Little birds sing out
Tweet, tweet, tweet
Look, Look. They're dancing on tiny feet

My special Bird.
What is that song?
Why do you sing to me
All the day long?

ASK LIT - TLE CHIP - PER HE KNOWS IT BEST

HE WROTE THE WORDS NOW AND YOU DO THE REST

Ask little Chipper
He knows it best
He wrote the words now
And you do the rest.

Come Little Rabbit
I love you
Come let me sing you
My song.

Chapter 6 Magical Days

Now Abbot's little group of four was complete, and they all loved it just the way it was. Abbot had a busy little mechanic, Builder of tunnels and writer of his song lyrics, who was Chipper; he had a wonderful musician, composer of his song, who was Bird; he had a sweet and quiet pet who was Rabbit.

After lunch he would sit with them and tell them stories, while they enjoyed the summer breeze in the warm sunshine. When their other friends heard about this then they too started to come to story time with Abbot.

Often to show their thanks flocks of birds would come and sing as a beautiful chorus, and this would make Rabbit smile.

Even if they were far apart, when Rabbit smiled first, then Abbot smiled, and when Abbot smiled first, then Rabbit smiled. They called it "YOU smile I smile". This was a magical thing and it never went away! Never!

Chapter 7 Rabbit, YOU are Magic!

Rabbit was trying very hard to keep his secret but it wasn't easy to do. He had so much fun with his new friends that sometimes he forgot to play little tricks on them - tricks that would make them laugh and would make Rabbit laugh too.

Once upon a time Abbot was a sad little boy - sad, because he spent much time without friends. But it was different now because he had his little group - Bird, Chipper, and Rabbit who would come and go but always be there in his thoughts.

They had many different activities during their vists together: lunch, storytelling, games, walks in the woods, walks by the pond, admiring flowers, coming back to rest, and taking a nap.

One day, while on a walk, Rabbit met two of his cousins who suggested they go to visit his grandmother who was preparing new jars of jelly at her home across the pond.

Rabbit loves jelly, but he loves Abbot even more than jelly, so he said to Abbot, "I'll be back when I've had enough jelly, but don't forget to look at the sun when it's a big ball low in the sky. I'll leave a message for you there. OK?" !

So Abbot smiled and said, "OK". Guess what Rabbit did? . . . Correct! He smiled! Then he jumped into a little boat with his cousins and they rowed away across the pond!

Now look at the picture and see what Abbot does every day that there's a big ball of sun low in the sky!

Where does Abbot look?

What does Abbot see?

What is Rabbit doing?

What happens to Abbot?

You are SO smart! Congratulations!

I think you enjoyed Abbot's Rabbit!

Did you?

CPSIA information can be obtained
at www.ICGtesting.com
Printed in the USA
LVOW06*0142031217
557218LV00009BA/19/P